Life is Lovely

Grace Young

As a reminder to all who read that life is filled with such simple, yet incredible joys

Appreciate everything and every moment

I step outside onto the patio after rain has heavily fallen and passed. The air smells of a fresh renewal and the greenery shines brighter than ever before. It is crisp, familiar, calming and refreshing.

Life is lovely.

After being outside in the cold December snow, I make a cup of hot chocolate and run a hot bath for myself. The bubbles smell of soothing lavender and my mug warms my hands and delights my senses with a peppermint touch.

Life is lovely.

I am in a room filled with people who I love and who love me in return. We are honest, inviting and we withhold nothing. Suddenly, laughter breaks out and I cannot stop. My stomach begins to sting from the giggles, yet my heart is warm and content.

Life is lovely.

It is a warm, June morning. Early, early morning. I can hear the birds singing as I walk along the beach, admiring the golden sun as it rises. Waves are crashing and dancing with one another.

Life is lovely.

You are walking down the street on a day that was simply too irresistibly beautiful to be inside. You are in good company with your favourite drink in hand, doing whatever you want and going where the day takes you.

Life is lovely.

A night in. Pants that fit just right. You are breathing deeply, watching your favourite movie and eating your favourite food.

Life is lovely.

You have just noticed someone across the room. Suddenly, your heart begins to bubble up at the thought of them. Without even having met them, you know that they are kind, and very loved. When you tell them that, they say it is exactly what they needed to hear that day.

Life is lovely.

Driving without a particular destination. Complete spontaneity with the people you love most. Random stops, laughter, sights to see and memories.

Life is lovely.

You are filled with joyful thoughts, sitting in a peacefully quiet place. No matter how hard you may try, you cannot hold back your smile. It gleams from ear to ear.

Life is lovely.

The feeling of fresh air blowing against your hands as you hold it outside of the car window. You let it swiftly cross your fingertips, and the sunlight caresses them.

Life is lovely.

Soft sounds of ukuleles and guitars. A bonfire that smells of the most natural and gentle earth. In the distance, the sun sets and the moon sits calmly on the lake.

Life is lovely.

Hearing that one voice that makes everything seem okay again.

Life is lovely.

Old crackling fireplace - inviting and strong. The mantel is filled with new photographs, and with every breath you take, you feel more at home.

Life is lovely.

Your toes are submerged in sea water. It is not too cold, but not too warm. Just right. The sunlight dances upon the waves.

Life is lovely.

Little coffee shops where the waitress knows your name, and everything is made with the most genuine care and love.

Life is lovely.

You find a random dock on the hottest day of the summer, and jump in it without hesitation. Fully clothed. Laughter is permeating through the air. You cannot stop smiling.

Life is lovely.

Meadows of the most beautiful pastel shades. Humming of birds, buzzing of pees. Harmony and peace surrounds you.

Life is lovely.

A long, deep breath outside after the hardest downpour you've seen in ages. The air is renewed with a fresh, crisp scent that makes every part of your spirit dance.

Life is lovely.

Tables with lace tablecloths, with ornate teapots, mugs and yellow napkins.

Life is lovely.

Laying in a field watching clouds pass by. In this moment, the world feels so silent and still. However, you are not lonely. For in this sky, you know there is something looking back. And you know that the supposed 'something', loves you.

Life is lovely.

A crowd waving lighters in unison, singing along to your favourite song. You realize that community is not as complex as it seems; it is merely brothers and sisters in this world enjoying their lives together.

Life is lovely.

An old, antique piano with chipped paint - yet it holds the most beautiful, triumphant notes you have ever heard.

Life is lovely.

Laughing after the drop of a roller-coaster, realizing that you are strong enough to withstand some of the craziest entertainment mechanisms the world has to offer.

Life is lovely.

The slightly uncomfortable stretchy feeling in your cheeks when you've been smiling for a long time.

Life is lovely.

Climbing to a rooftop to watch a sunrise.

Life is lovely.

You have been travelling by car all day. You finally make it home, after barely being able to keep your eyes open - you crawl into bed and instantly drift into a deep, comforting sleep.

Life is lovely.

Sand on your toes, sun on your face, and a gentle breeze that dances with you in a way you can't explain.

Life is lovely.

A record player that amplifies a beautiful, crackly song from the 1940's.

Life is lovely.

The feeling when a powerful sentence is uttered, and there is a moment of silence before an eruption of applause.

Life is lovely.

How good your voice sounds when you sing in the shower.

Life is lovely.

Words of wisdom from a seven year-old.

Life is lovely.

Hiking with your friend, who is unashamed to look back and grab your hand so that you get across safely.

Life is lovely.

Driving past an untouched field of greenery. The smell, the feeling of the air, and the sight of rich emerald and fullness of nature.

Life is lovely.

Starting a book and falling in love with it on the first page.

Life is lovely.

A young child looking at you with arms in the air, admiring you as a safe place and someone they want to be close to.

Life is lovely.

Those talks with friends late at night that spill over into the morning.

Life is lovely.

The silent pride in losing your voice the day after going to a concert.

Life is lovely.

Bike riding at dawn.

Life is lovely.

A crowd clapping in complete, perfect unison.

Life is lovely.

Taking a day to take care of yourself.

Life is lovely.

People who are genuinely funny.

Life is lovely.

Bright colours blending together to create a palette of happiness.

Life is lovely.

Holding pinkies.

Life is lovely.

Old, rustic golden picture frames.

Life is lovely.

Dancing in the kitchen, after a good nights rest.

Life is lovely.

Baskets full of daisies, lilacs and dandelions.

Life is lovely.

A cup of tea to soothe your mind and body.

Life is lovely.

Checking the final task off of your 'to-do' list.

Life is lovely.

Road trips with no destination in mind.

Life is lovely.

Filled sketchbooks and notebooks that have been completed with the power of your own mind.

Life is lovely.

Old churches, wooden pews, happy people.

Life is lovely.

People who make intentional eye-contact with you while you're speaking.

Life is lovely.

Sore feet from dancing and jumping.

Life is lovely.

Crazy December blizzard-watching from the comfort of your cozy living room.

Life is lovely.

Fingers with dainty rings.

Life is lovely.

The feeling after you try something completely new, and realize it wasn't that scary after all.

Life is lovely.

The words 'Dear,' 'Precious', 'Exquisite', and 'Delicate'.

Life is lovely.

Realizing the beauty of your truest self.

Life is lovely.

A day so blissfully busy that you don't have time to be on your phone.

Life is lovely.

Yellow shoes.

Life is lovely.

Apple picking in a cool, gentle fall, with the people that you love most.

Life is lovely.

Counteracting thoughts of 'what if you can't do it?'
with thoughts of 'what if I can?'

Life is lovely.

Tap dancers.

Life is lovely.

The way sun shines off of the beautiful hair on your head.

Life is lovely.

Being complimented on your personality in a way you haven't heard before.

Life is lovely.

Walking next to a rumbling river as the sun rises; completely calmed and aware.

Life is lovely.

Birds chirping with each other.

Life is lovely.

Baking something for yourself, just because.

Life is lovely.

Realizing that the change you were so worried about is actually better for you in the end.

Life is lovely.

Clear blue seas, gentle waves.

Life is lovely.

*Sitting next to a window during a thunderstorm
with your favourite adventure buddy.*

Life is lovely.

Intricate lettering on an envelope addressed to you.

Life is lovely.

Listening to your favourite music before bed.

Life is lovely.

Taking a walk by yourself first thing in the morning.

Life is lovely.

*Scheduling a day to take care of yourself
intentionally.*

Life is lovely.

Accepting that who you are is first loved.

Life is lovely.

The people who aren't afraid to dance in public with you.

Life is lovely.

Soft, calming music.

Life is lovely.

A heart for helping others.

Life is lovely.

Sunday morning.

Life is lovely.

Stepping on crunchy leaves.

Life is lovely.

Dipping your toes in the water.

Life is lovely.

The beauty of excitement.

Life is lovely.

In a room with dozens of people there, there's someone who cares most to talk to you.

Life is lovely.

Flower petals.

Life is lovely.

Smiley-faced scribbles on lined paper.

Life is lovely.

Loving someone more than you love yourself.

Life is lovely.

Friendly dogs.

Life is lovely.

Soft blankets on a cold day.

Life is lovely.

Checkered dance floors.

Life is lovely.

Morning light reflecting from the window onto a wooden floor.

Life is lovely.

The sound of a choir harmonizing.

Life is lovely.

Hands covered in paint.

Life is lovely.

Chalk-painted desks.

Life is lovely.

Birch trees dressed with singing birds.

Life is lovely.

Bright-coloured umbrellas and dancing in the rain.

Life is lovely.

Hitting the high note (or at least trying to) while singing in the shower.

Life is lovely.

Patio-conversations with people who ask good questions.

Life is lovely.

*The relief of biking down a hill after pushing
yourself up it.*

Life is lovely.

Root-beer floats.

Life is lovely.

Cozy socks and big sweaters.

Life is lovely.

Putting in time to invest in creativity.

Life is lovely.

Yoga mats and tall candles.

Life is lovely.

Watercolour flowers.

Life is lovely.

Ice cream cones on the first day of summer.

Life is lovely.

Remembering that there is only one you *in the history of the universe.*

Life is lovely.

Talking to people who were alive when the massive tree in your park was planted.

Life is lovely.

Socks with ruffles and red shoes.

Life is lovely.

Breathing deeply when you need a moment to yourself.

Life is lovely.

Hugging someone who needs it.

Life is lovely.

Porcelain teapots, cups and saucers.

Life is lovely.

Being called 'dashing'.

Life is lovely.

Stepping away from a situation to remind yourself of the beauty that ever touches the earth.

Life is lovely.

Accepting your ability to change the world.

Life is lovely.

Hearing someone playing guitar outside.

Life is lovely.

Tender hearts.

Life is lovely.

YOU
DID
IT !

You just read One Hundred and Ten things that make life even more fun and colourful.

FROM THE AUTHOR

I wrote Life is Lovely because I was so captivated by the small glimpses of glory in each day. I began to write these things down as they came to me because it was so evident to me that in just acknowledging the beauty that ever surrounds us, we can shine a light within our own lives and in the lives of others.

So, my friends, it goes to show you that no matter what you're facing, life will never be able to take away the glory that's been handed to us and freely given. It is simply ours.

Your life, your soul and personality contains sunshine that cannot be put out.

Your smile breaks chains of darkness and holds a torch of freedom.

You are a world changer! Live in that truth!